THE GENIUS KID'S GUIDE TO SHARKS

BY ETHAN PEMBROKE

North Star
KIDS

TABLE OF CONTENTS

SHARK FACTS

There are many creatures swimming through the world's oceans. They come in all sizes, and there are countless species. Many can be harmful, but few are more feared than the shark.

There are hundreds of shark species, but they all share common features. Sharks have skeletons made of cartilage rather than bone. They are predatory creatures. Most sharks are carnivores.

The basking shark is truly one of the masters of the sea. It is the second-largest fish in the world. Few animals try to challenge this massive sea monster.

Basking sharks have a nose that is slightly upturned.

The basking shark is also known as the elephant shark, the bone shark, and the sailfish.

Even with all of its strength, the basking shark is a very gentle creature. Basking sharks prefer to glide through the ocean. They feast on plankton and bask in the sun.

WHAT THEY LOOK LIKE

Basking sharks are a grayish-brown color. Their bodies are long and cylindrical. They have pointy snouts, big eyes, and many rows of small teeth. All of these features make a distinct creature.

These sharks can get up to 40 feet (12 m) long. They can weigh more than 5 tons (4.5 t). An adult basking shark's mouth can be 3 feet (0.9 m) wide.

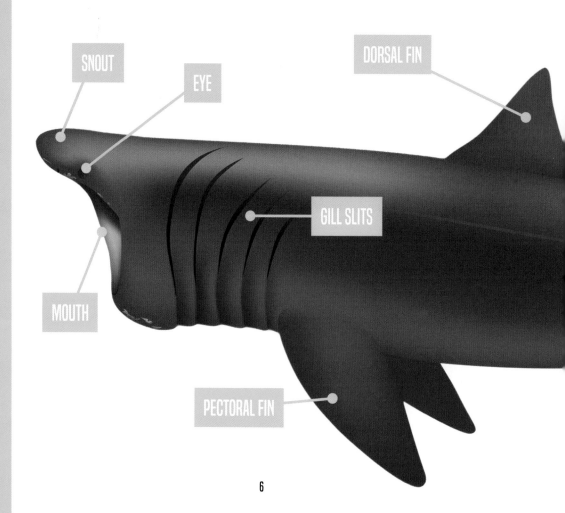

SNOUT

EYE

DORSAL FIN

GILL SLITS

MOUTH

PECTORAL FIN

Basking sharks have rough skin.

Another unusual feature of the basking shark is its broad gills. A basking shark's gill slits almost completely surround its head. They are used for breathing and also assist in eating. A shark's tail fin is also called a caudal fin.

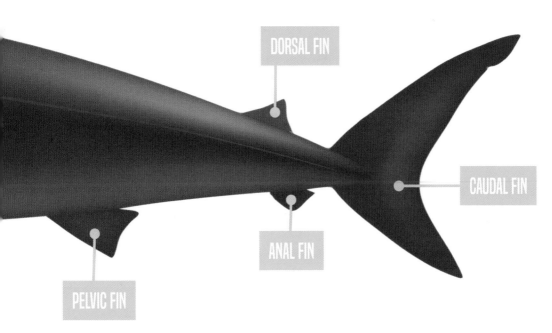

DORSAL FIN

CAUDAL FIN

ANAL FIN

PELVIC FIN

WHERE THEY LIVE

Basking sharks live in moderate and cold waters worldwide. They migrate with the seasons. These sharks travel thousands of miles seeking comfortable water temperature and looking for food.

Basking sharks move at a slow 3 miles per hour (5 kmh). They usually travel alone or in groups of two to three. But schools of 500 basking sharks have been reported.

WHERE DO BASKING SHARKS LIVE?

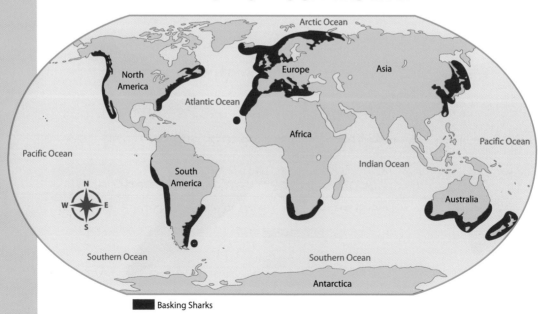

Basking Sharks

When temperatures are warmer, basking sharks migrate north. In cooler months, they go south.

Basking sharks can be found at the surface of the ocean. A basking shark cruises along with its back and first dorsal fin sticking out of the water. Some people think the sharks look like they are sunning themselves. This is how the basking shark got its name.

A basking shark can also dive very deep. The species has been spotted up to 3,280 feet (1,000 m) below the water's surface. This is a big range for a shark to live in.

FOOD

Basking sharks do not usually hunt for their meals. Instead, they swim through the water with their mouths open. As they swim, small fish, plankton, larvae, and other creatures collect in their massive mouths. This food gets caught in their gill rakers. The gill rakers strain the food from the water. Then, the water is pushed out through the gills. A basking shark's gill rakers filter about 2,000 tons (1,800 t) of water per hour.

A basking shark catches plankton.

Gill rakers are bristles similar to teeth that are inside the gill slits. These gill rakers filter the basking shark's food from the water.

In the winter, the basking shark sheds its gill rakers. What happens to the shark while it regrows its gill rakers is mostly unknown. Some people think that the shark lives off of fat stored in its liver. Others believe that the shark looks for food at the bottom of the ocean.

Still, the shark survives until its gill rakers grow back. After regrowth, the shark returns to the water's surface to bask again.

SENSES

Sharks need to figure out their surroundings while traveling. Sharks use their senses of smell and hearing often. This is especially true when traveling over long distances and while hunting.

A shark uses its sense of smell to identify objects. Odorants wash into a shark's nasal sac and tell the shark what is nearby.

There is one sense that is unique to sharks and their relatives. Sharks have small pores on their bodies called ampullae of Lorenzini. These pores sense electrical fields in the water. All living creatures produce an electrical charge. Sharks use the ampullae of Lorenzini to locate their prey.

Basking sharks have small eyes, but they have many other senses to help them survive.

Basking sharks have large mouths.

BABIES

Little is known about how a basking shark reproduces. When a female shark is between 12 and 16 years old, she is ready to mate. After mating, eggs inside the female become fertilized. Basking sharks are believed to carry their young for about three years.

The young develop inside the female basking shark. The embryos survive until birth by feeding off of the remaining eggs and other unborn sharks.

Scientists still don't know everything about basking shark reproduction.

A shark's liver helps it float.

Baby sharks are called pups. Scientists aren't sure how many pups a female basking shark can give birth to. One basking shark gave birth to five live pups. When they are born, the pups swim away. They are fully developed and ready to care for themselves.

Basking shark pups are the largest fish babies in the world. They can be 6 feet (2 m) long at birth. Like many large shark species, basking sharks grow very slowly. It takes many years for a basking shark to reach its full size.

ATTACK AND DEFENSE

Few animals would even try to hunt a basking shark because of its great size. But this does not mean that they are always safe. In many countries, people hunt basking sharks. They are killed for their oil, fins, skins, and meat.

A basking shark's fins are used for shark fin soup. Its liver is used for oil. The basking shark's liver accounts for about 25 percent of its total weight and is very valuable. In the 1700s and 1800s, the oil was used in lamps. Today, there are many uses for shark oil, but most are for medicinal purposes.

Since basking sharks are often near the water's surface, people might see them while swimming.

Basking sharks aren't considered dangerous to people. However, they can still hurt people because they are such large animals.

Basking sharks also have to deal with parasites. Sea lampreys use basking sharks for transportation. These creatures attach themselves to the shark's skin and are an annoyance. Sometimes, people see basking sharks leap out of the water to shake off parasites.

SHARK FACTS

Common sawsharks, also known as longnose sawsharks, are easily recognized by their long, blade-like snouts. This feature can seem strange and awkward, but sawsharks are fascinating and special animals.

Sharks normally spend their time alone. But sawsharks are known to form schools.

People are still trying to learn more about the ocean's many creatures.

Common sawsharks present little danger to humans. Sawsharks are not known to kill people. Sharks are only interested in finding meals that they are familiar with. They do not naturally prey on humans.

WHAT THEY LOOK LIKE

The common sawshark's flattened, blade-like snout is its most distinct feature. Long barbels hang from the underside of the snout. The snout is studded with both long and short teeth. The teeth are replaced when they are broken or lost.

Sawsharks have flat, slender bodies. They can grow to be 5 feet (1.5 m) in length.

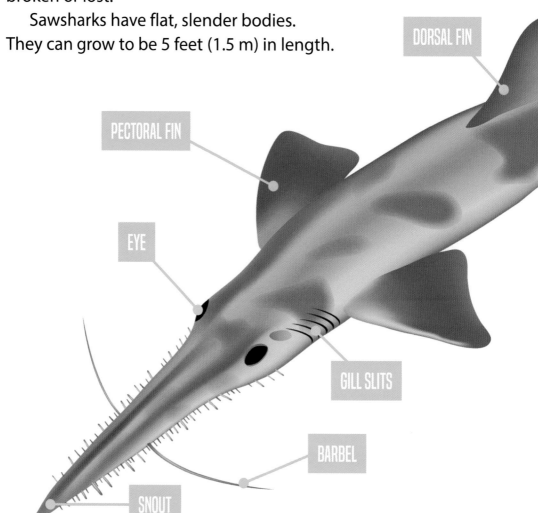

DORSAL FIN

PECTORAL FIN

EYE

GILL SLITS

BARBEL

SNOUT

Like many shark species, female sawsharks are longer than the males.

The common sawshark has two dorsal fins, and it has five gill slits on each side of its head. It has a small mouth that rests behind its long snout. The sawshark's back is covered with dark spots and blotches. Its belly is a beige or yellowish color.

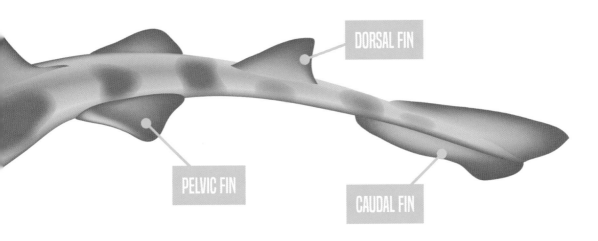

DORSAL FIN

PELVIC FIN

CAUDAL FIN

The common sawshark has 19 to 25 teeth on either side of its snout.

WHERE THEY LIVE

The common sawshark is a temperate and subtropical Australian species. It lives in the eastern Indian Ocean along the Australian and Tasmanian coasts. The common sawshark is found along continental shelves.

Common sawsharks are shallow-water creatures. Their bodies are adapted to living near the bottom of the ocean. Their flat forms allow them to get close to the ground.

Sawsharks choose sandy areas to live in. During the day, they remain motionless on the seafloor. At night, they venture out to hunt. They dig through the sand, algae, and seaweed to find food.

WHERE DO COMMON SAWSHARKS LIVE?

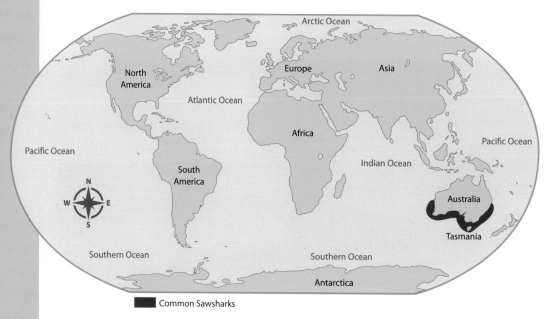

Common Sawsharks

Australia's marine habitat supports a lot of life.

FOOD

Sawsharks eat many different types of creatures. They feed on squid and small fish such as gapers and cornetfish. They also find crustaceans that are traveling on the ground. These creatures become tasty meals for sawsharks.

Cornetfish are long and thin.

The common sawshark trails its barbels along the seafloor to find its prey.

A common sawshark uses its barbels as feelers to detect prey hidden in the sand. The sawshark swipes back and forth with its snout to dig up the creatures. Then, the sawshark disables its prey by hitting it with sideways swipes.

SENSES

Sharks have the same five senses that humans have. They also have special senses that are adapted for their environments. For example, sharks can detect pressure changes in the water. This allows them to determine water depth and which way is up.

Sharks also have a lateral line sense system. Along each side of a shark's body are two sensory tubes that are the lateral lines. The lateral lines pick up vibrations in the water. These vibrations, as well as the electrical currents, will lead a shark to its next meal.

Large sharks will hunt sawsharks.

Humans fish for and kill many types of sharks.

With their many senses, sawsharks can search out prey and avoid predators. Without the extra help, they would have difficulty surviving in the dark ocean.

BABIES

Developing sharks grow inside of the mother common sawshark. The babies are contained and protected in egg sacs. As they mature, the unborn sharks live off of nutrition in the eggs.

It takes around one year for the unborn sharks to develop. So, when they are born they are ready to survive on their own.

Mother common sawsharks give birth to between three and 22 young. The pups are born with the larger set of teeth on their snouts. The teeth are soft and lie flat during birth. The blades eventually straighten and harden. Smaller blades fill in between the larger ones.

A common sawshark embryo

The long snout makes sawsharks easy to identify.

ATTACK AND DEFENSE

Most sharks are carnivores. They eat live prey. In addition to being hunters, many sharks are hunted for their meat. Many people find the meat to be a delicacy. The shark's skin is made into leather, and its teeth are sold as souvenirs.

Some people eat shark meat.

Sawsharks can live to be about 15 years old.

A shark's best defense against predators is to hide. This is especially true for small or young sharks. The pups survive by remaining in nursery areas. Here, they feed on prey suited to their sizes. Their skin colorings keep them hidden.

The common sawshark's blade-like snout is its best defensive tool. If caught in a net, this shark can seriously harm a human attempting to free it. And with a few sideways swipes, the teeth on the snout can disable a creature.

SHARK FACTS

One of the most feared sharks is the great white. It is a large, active, powerful shark. The great white is a rare fish. Yet it is responsible for a number of attacks on humans. This makes the great white the most dangerous shark to people.

Some divers stay in cages for their own protection while looking at sharks.

The great white shark is a fearsome predator.

However, many attacks on humans aren't deadly. Researchers have found that great white sharks are very curious. When they bite people, it is known as sample biting. Sharks are just trying to figure out what it is. They usually let go of their human victims. However, people can still be seriously injured by a great white shark's bite.

WHAT THEY LOOK LIKE

The great white shark is shaped like a torpedo. Its pointed snout contains powerful jaws filled with large teeth. Each tooth has a saw-like edge for cutting prey.

This fearsome shark has large pectoral and dorsal fins and a strong caudal fin. Two pelvic fins are located toward the shark's rear. Behind those is an anal fin used to keep the great white stable while swimming. Five gill slits are on each side of the head.

Adult great whites can grow more than 20 feet (6 m) long. They can weigh 4,000 pounds (1,800 kg) or more. Females are larger than males.

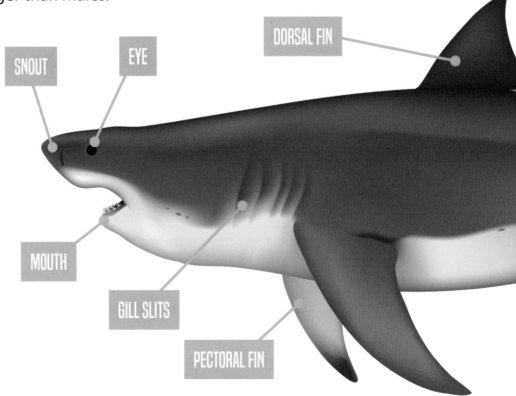

DORSAL FIN

SNOUT

EYE

MOUTH

GILL SLITS

PECTORAL FIN

The great white shark belongs to the family *Lamnidae*.

The great white shark is named for its white belly. Its back and sides are dark blue, gray, or brown. This coloring camouflages the shark whether viewed from below or above.

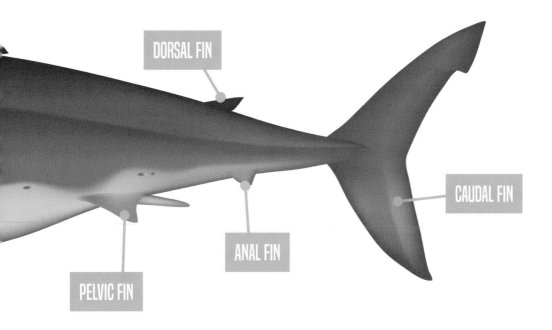

DORSAL FIN

CAUDAL FIN

ANAL FIN

PELVIC FIN

WHERE THEY LIVE

Great white sharks live in temperate oceans around the world. They can be found near the surface or in deep water. Scientists have tracked great whites diving around 3,000 feet (900 m) below the surface.

Usually, great whites swim along coastlines, but some are found far offshore. Research shows one great white traveled from South Africa to Australia and back again. That's a distance of 12,000 miles (19,300 km). The trip took just nine months.

WHERE DO GREAT WHITE SHARKS LIVE?

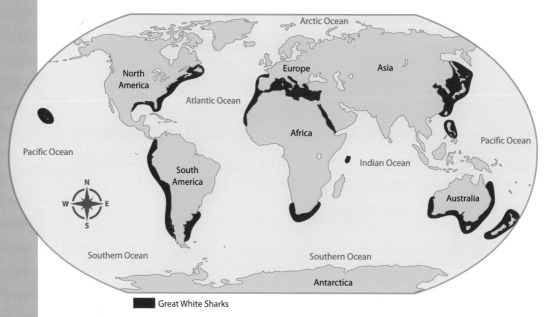

Arctic Ocean

North America

Europe

Asia

Atlantic Ocean

Africa

Pacific Ocean

Indian Ocean

Pacific Ocean

South America

Australia

N
W E
S

Southern Ocean

Southern Ocean

Antarctica

◼ Great White Sharks

Scientists aren't sure how many great white sharks there are.

Compared with other shark species, the great white is rarely seen or caught. Little is known about its social behavior. However, research shows this shark usually swims alone and occasionally travels in pairs.

FOOD

The great white shark is the largest predatory fish on Earth. It has a few rows of sharp teeth. A great white can have around 300 triangular teeth in its mouth. It can eat around 22,000 pounds (9,980 kg) of food each year.

Great white sharks are known to jump out of the water to catch prey.

Great whites have large teeth.

Great whites feed on a variety of sea creatures. Young great whites eat fish and other sharks. As they grow, their diets change. They begin eating bigger, more active prey. Larger great whites eat porpoises, dolphins, sea lions, and small whales. Great whites may also feed on dead animals such as whales and basking sharks.

SENSES

The great white's well-developed senses allow it to navigate its underwater world. They also help make this shark a fearsome hunter.

   The great white has good eyesight. In fact, it is the only fish known to exhibit a behavior called spyhopping. The great white lifts its

The great white can smell a single drop of blood in 25 gallons (95 L) of water.

Great white sharks can look intimidating to many people.

head out of the water. This way, it can examine its surroundings. The great white also has excellent senses of smell and hearing.

Special sense organs allow great whites to detect electric fields. Sensing these fields allows great whites to find prey and mates. Sharks also have a sensitive lateral line system for detecting prey.

BABIES

Some studies have estimated that great whites do not begin breeding until they are around age 25 or 30. Scientists believe female great whites are pregnant for about 12 months. The pups are born live after they hatch from eggs

Young great whites snack on rays.

A single dorsal fin can strike fear in the hearts of many people.

inside the mother. The mother gives birth to two to 12 pups every two to three years. The newborn sharks are more than 3 feet (1 m) long.

The mother leaves her pups to survive on their own. The ocean is a harsh place for newborn sharks. Many great whites do not live past the first year.

ATTACK AND DEFENSE

The great white is one of the most powerful predators of the sea. It hunts by surprising its prey and delivering a forceful, fatal bite. The shark then retreats and waits for its prey to die before returning to feed.

Great whites are at the top of the marine food chain. They have few natural predators. Orca whales may hunt great whites.

Great white sharks will catch and eat seals.

Divers must treat great whites with respect.

The great white's most dangerous enemies are humans. This shark's jaws and teeth are valuable. Humans also hunt the great white for the food its meat provides.

This shark's population numbers may be in danger from humans. Today, many people are working to protect great whites from overfishing. Countries such as South Africa, the United States, and Australia protect these amazing creatures.

SHARK FACTS

There are ten species of hammerhead sharks. They are named for their hammer-shaped heads. These unusual shapes serve many purposes for these interesting creatures.

Most hammerhead sharks are not dangerous to humans. However, two species, great and smooth hammerheads, are aggressive. These large sharks are considered dangerous to humans.

Hammerhead sharks can live around 20 to 30 years.

Even though hammerheads are endangered, people still fish for them.

Great hammerhead sharks are endangered. They do not give birth to young often. People are also threatening this species. They catch and kill them. Today, some people are trying to protect these sharks so they don't go extinct.

WHAT THEY LOOK LIKE

The hammerhead's body is perfectly designed to move through its underwater world. The shark's many fins help it swim with ease.

The flattened head is called a cephalofoil. Its shape varies by species. For example, the great hammerhead has a rectangular head. The bonnethead has a head shaped like a shovel.

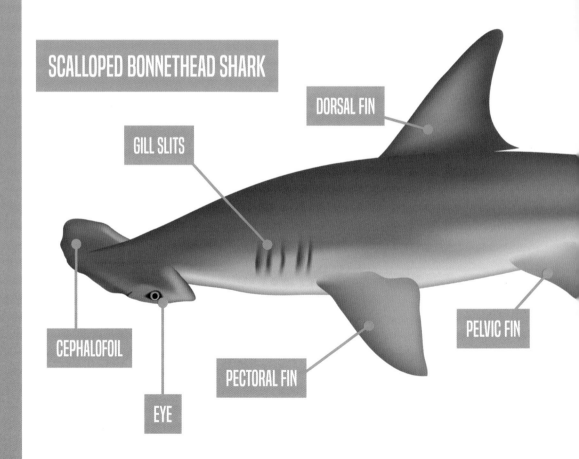

SCALLOPED BONNETHEAD SHARK

DORSAL FIN

GILL SLITS

CEPHALOFOIL

EYE

PECTORAL FIN

PELVIC FIN

Bonnethead shark

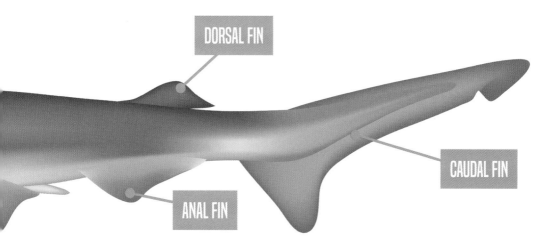

DORSAL FIN

CAUDAL FIN

ANAL FIN

Size also varies among the species. The 3-foot- (1-m) long scalloped bonnethead is the smallest. At 20 feet (6 m), the great hammerhead is the largest.

All hammerheads are gray or brown along their backs and sides. The bellies are white. Each hammerhead has five pairs of gill slits along the sides of the head.

WHERE THEY LIVE

Hammerhead sharks live in temperate and tropical oceans around the world. A hammerhead's habitat varies by species. In general, hammerheads swim in shallow coastal waters or above continental shelves. They may also be found far offshore.

Many hammerhead species swim alone, but some form schools. The bonnethead is often seen in groups of up to 15. The scalloped hammerhead is the only big hammerhead species known to form large schools.

WHERE DO HAMMERHEAD SHARKS LIVE?

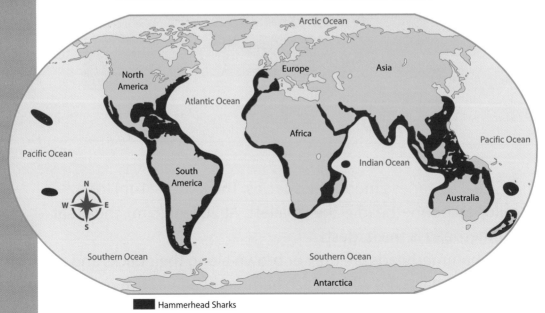

Arctic Ocean

Europe

Asia

North America

Atlantic Ocean

Africa

Pacific Ocean

Pacific Ocean

Indian Ocean

South America

Australia

N
W   E
S

Southern Ocean

Southern Ocean

Antarctica

▬ Hammerhead Sharks

Some schools have been known to have hundreds of scalloped hammerheads.

Seasonally, some hammerhead shark species migrate. During the winter, they move toward the equator where the water is warmer. They travel toward the poles during the summer.

FOOD

Most hammerheads feed in shallow water along coasts. They eat a variety of prey such as bony fish, squid, lobsters, and crabs. Larger hammerheads also feed on small sharks and bottom-dwelling fish.

Hammerhead sharks often hunt alone.

Bonnethead sharks love to eat blue crabs.

Stingrays are a favorite meal for great hammerheads. In fact, these sharks are known to eat stingrays whole. This includes the poisonous tail spine. A shark may feast on a large meal every two or three days.

SENSES

A hammerhead shark uses its oddly shaped head to its advantage. A round eye is located on each end of the head. This gives the shark a better range of vision than many other shark species.

The shark's large head helps it find food.

The skin around a shark's head and the front end of its body is covered with sense organs. They sense the electric fields of living animals. The hammerhead shark's large head surface provides more area for these organs. This, along with its lateral line system, helps a hammerhead shark easily find prey.

BABIES

Hammerhead reproduction varies from species to species. The number of pups a mother has ranges from two to 42. The smaller species produce fewer young than the larger species.

Hammerheads often give birth to pups in the spring or summer.

Young hammerheads live in shallow waters along the coast.

A female bonnethead is pregnant for five months. She gives birth to four to 14 pups. The pups are around 14 inches (35 cm) long.

A great hammerhead mother carries her young for 11 months. She gives birth to six to 42 pups. The pups can be 20 to 27 inches (50 to 70 cm) long.

Pregnant hammerheads give birth to live pups in shallow, protected coastal waters. Then, the mothers swim away. Left on their own, the pups use their well-developed senses to survive.

ATTACK AND DEFENSE

Hammerhead sharks are skilled hunters. They have many rows of teeth to catch prey. There are several rows of new teeth below the working teeth. When a tooth is lost or damaged, a new one replaces it.

The teeth of smaller hammerhead species, such as bonnetheads, are thick and flattened. These teeth are suited to crushing the shellfish they prey on.

Since most hammerheads are small, they aren't dangerous to people.

Sometimes people hunt
hammerheads for their teeth.

Larger hammerheads have huge, blade-like teeth. A bigger hammerhead also uses its head to attack prey. Using its large cephalofoil, the shark rams and pins prey.

Hammerhead sharks can also become prey. Smaller hammerheads rely on their senses to avoid large bony fish and other sharks. Large adult hammerheads have almost nothing to fear except humans. Humans hunt hammerheads for food and products such as vitamins and leather.

SHARK FACTS

A ghostly glow can be seen deep in the ocean. It appears far beyond where most people travel. Curious fish notice the glow and want to find out more. They have to get closer.

A small fish swims up to the source. This is a dangerous choice. Behind the glow is a lantern shark. And it is too late for the fish

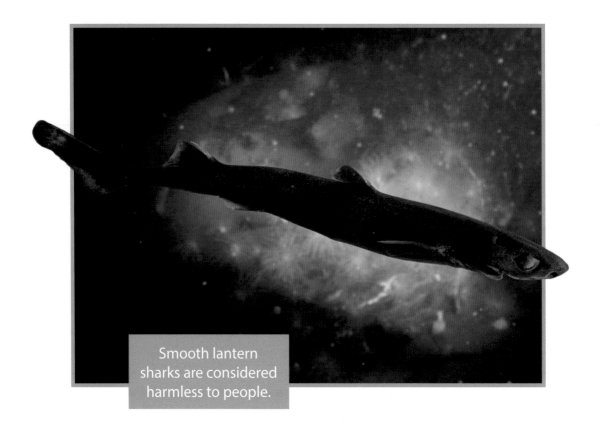

Smooth lantern sharks are considered harmless to people.

Moller's lantern shark

to escape. Like all sharks, lantern sharks are predatory fish.

The mysteries of the lantern shark are as amazing as its glow. These tiny sharks live deep in the ocean where there is little light. They have adapted unusual ways to survive the cold temperatures and darkness of their environments.

WHAT THEY LOOK LIKE

There are many species of lantern sharks. But all lantern sharks share similar traits. They can be easily identified.

Lantern sharks are dark brown or black. They have long tails. There is a large spine in front of each of the two dorsal fins on their backs.

Lantern sharks have big eyes. This trait is common in deep-sea animals. Lantern sharks also have flat snouts and small mouths. And they are covered with scales called dermal denticles. These scales are tiny and tooth-like. Lantern sharks are some of the smallest sharks on the planet. The dwarf lantern shark is the smallest of the lantern sharks.

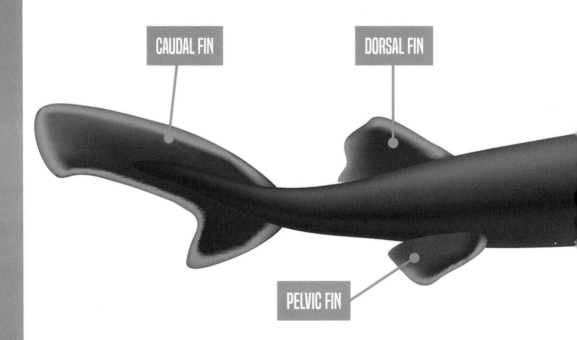

CAUDAL FIN

DORSAL FIN

PELVIC FIN

Pygmy sharks are small.

Adults measure only around 8 inches (20 cm) long. The great lantern shark is one of the largest in this species. Some can be around 28 inches (70 cm) long. Like many other sharks, females grow larger than males.

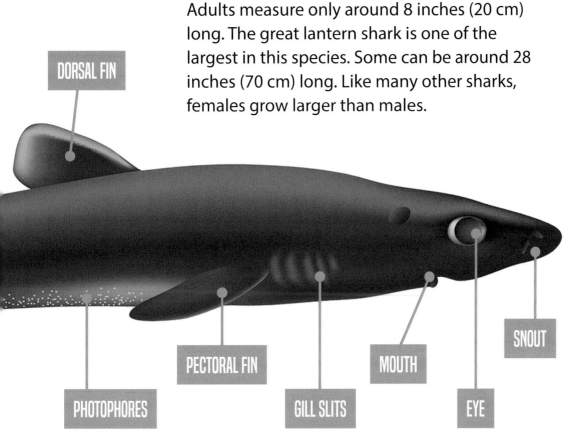

DORSAL FIN

PHOTOPHORES

PECTORAL FIN

GILL SLITS

MOUTH

EYE

SNOUT

WHERE THEY LIVE

Lantern sharks live in almost every ocean. They are found in the Atlantic Ocean from Scandinavia all the way to South Africa. They live in the deep waters near Japan, Taiwan, and China. They are also found in the South Pacific Ocean and the Mediterranean Sea.

The ocean floor has as much variety as dry land. There are valleys and mountains. There are places with a lot of life and areas that are barren. Temperatures also change from area to area.

A new species of lantern shark was found in 2015 near Central America. It's called the ninja lantern shark. It has been

WHERE DO LANTERN SHARKS LIVE?

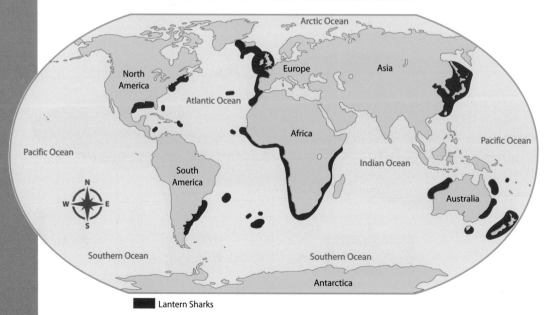

Lantern Sharks

found between 2,700 and 4,700 feet (820 and 1,430 m) below the surface.

Deep ocean water has unusual features. There is almost no light, which means there are fewer plants. Most deepwater sharks are fairly inactive. So, lantern sharks use less energy than sharks closer to the surface. Lantern sharks survive well in these conditions. Their dark bodies blend into their surroundings. And they have special senses and traits that help them stay alive.

Some people explore underwater worlds with special diving equipment, but even they can't go to the depths where lantern sharks live.

FOOD

Lantern sharks live off of crustaceans, smaller fish, and squid. Because these sharks live in deep waters, this food can be scarce. So, lantern sharks use their natural abilities to make finding food easier.

The lantern shark's large eyes help it see prey in the dark ocean waters.

Some young lantern sharks eat krill.

Hunting in the sea is hard work. When hunting, lantern sharks draw their prey out of the darkness with their glowing lights. It is important for sharks to get the food that they need. Without it they will not have the energy to escape danger or capture another meal.

SENSES

Recognizing the shape of a lantern shark is a good way to identify one. However, what really makes a lantern shark different is its glow.

On a lantern shark's belly, and sometimes in its mouth, are organs called photophores. The photophores give off light by a chemical reaction.

Lantern sharks aren't the only fish that lights up. Anglerfish (pictured) can glow, too.

The glow that the lantern shark gives off is called bioluminescence. It is not unique to this shark. Bioluminescence is what makes a firefly glow.

The light the lantern shark gives off is used for finding food and for communicating with other sharks. The light is very important to the lantern shark's survival.

Other senses are vital to sharks. They have good eyesight and strong senses of smell. They can also sense other animals in the water by the vibrations that the creatures make.

BABIES

Some people believe that the lights on a lantern shark are used to attract a mate. But there are many unknown things about the mating process. Lantern sharks live so deep in the ocean that it can be difficult to study them.

Female lantern sharks do not lay eggs like many other fish. Instead, the lantern shark's pups remain in the mother even after they hatch. After a short time, the mother gives birth and the pups enter the water. The litter size varies between species.

There are many things people don't know about ocean creatures.

A man holds a captured velvet belly lantern shark and an embryo.

The smooth lantern shark has been known to have eight to 18 pups. Ninja lantern sharks are thought to have around five pups.

   Mother lantern sharks do not take care of their pups after they are birthed. The pups swim off as soon as they are born. With luck, they will survive.

ATTACK AND DEFENSE

Sharks normally have few predators. In fact, humans and other sharks are their most common enemies.

The lantern shark's glow helps it blend into the dim light coming from above.

Unlike many shark species, lantern sharks are not fished commercially. But they are small, so they have many larger sharks to fear.

The lantern shark's dark color helps it remain hidden when necessary. This is its

main form of defense against large predators. Some lantern sharks have another defense— their spines. These sharp spines injure the mouth of the animal that tries to eat it.

Lantern sharks need to keep an eye out for predators in the ocean.

SHARK FACTS

Mako sharks are fast, focused, and hungry. They are one of the most effective predators in the ocean. Mako sharks are sleek and powerful animals. Their bodies are made for speed and endurance.

Shortfin makos are also known as blue pointers.

Shortfin makos grow fast compared with some other shark species.

There are two species of mako sharks. The shortfin mako is the most common. Little is known about the longfin mako. But many similarities exist between the two species.

Mako sharks are some of the fastest fish in the ocean. Shortfin mako sharks cruise through the water at about 45 miles per hour (72 kmh). When necessary, a mako can burst up to much greater speeds.

WHAT THEY LOOK LIKE

Mako sharks have slender blue-gray bodies that appear deep blue in the water. But their bellies are white. Mako sharks have long, pointed snouts. Their tails are crescent shaped to assist in swimming.

The shortfin mako has large, round, black eyes. The eyes of a longfin mako are even larger. Longfin makos also have larger pectoral fins.

An average male shortfin mako is between 6.5 and 7 feet (2 to 2.1 m) long. Females are about 9 to 9.5 feet (2.7 to 3 m) long. Large shortfin makos can weigh more than 1,000 pounds (450 kg) and are longer than 12 feet (4 m).

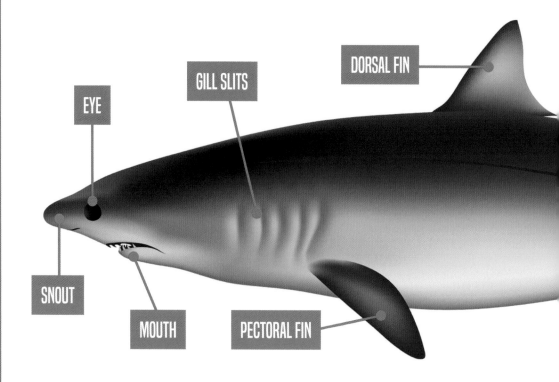

DORSAL FIN

GILL SLITS

EYE

SNOUT

MOUTH

PECTORAL FIN

Makos have long teeth.

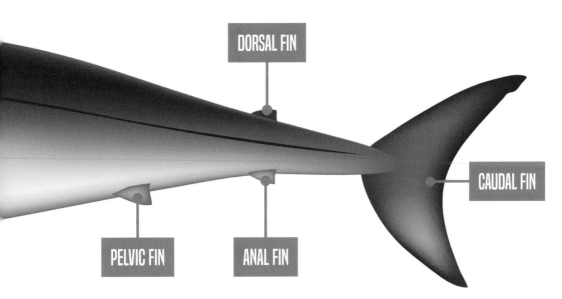

DORSAL FIN

CAUDAL FIN

PELVIC FIN

ANAL FIN

WHERE THEY LIVE

Mako sharks can be found worldwide. Usually they stay in temperate and tropical waters. They prefer water that is between 63 and 68 degrees Fahrenheit (17 and 20°C).

Makos are active sharks. They migrate seasonally to warmer waters. Besides changes in water temperatures, sharks migrate because of food availability. Some sharks migrate when they are ready to reproduce.

The distance a shark travels depends on its species. Some sharks simply move to different water depths. Others may travel 100 to 1,000 miles (160 to 1,600 km). Mako sharks are fantastic swimmers. They can dive up to 500 feet (150 m) deep.

WHERE DO MAKO SHARKS LIVE?

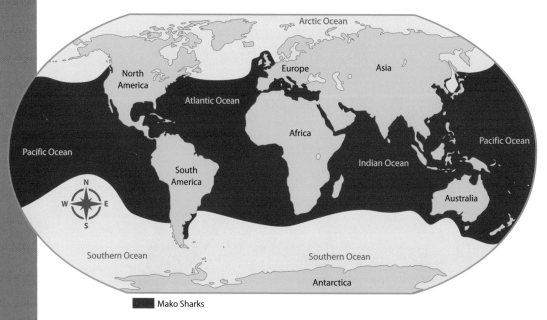

■ Mako Sharks

But they spend most of their time close to the water's surface. Makos are also able to leap out of the water. They can rush toward the surface and jump more than 20 feet (6 m) into the air.

Mako sharks are often seen with their large dorsal fins sticking out of the water.

FOOD

Mako sharks use all of their abilities to hunt. Their senses help them find food from far away. Their speed allows them to swim quickly toward prey. Their long, blade-like teeth help them swiftly kill their prey.

Fishermen will trick makos in order to catch them.

Tuna is a favorite meal for makos.

Shortfin makos eat many types of fish. They feast on tuna, swordfish, mackerel, sturgeon, and squid. They will eat other sharks, too. Makos generally leave sea mammals alone, but sometimes they eat dolphins. They also eat sea turtles. Not much is safe from a hungry mako.

Mako sharks have a special hunting method. They chase down their prey and bite it hard. Then, they swallow their victims whole. If this does not work, the mako bites off the prey's tail. This makes the creature easier to catch because it cannot swim.

SENSES

Mako sharks have well-developed senses for hunting. They have good vision, and they sense vibrations made by other creatures. Makos also have an incredibly sensitive sense of smell.

Mako sharks can detect the body fluids of injured or distressed animals in the water.

Only a trained professional should get close to a mako shark.

Like other fish, mako sharks have a lateral line system. So, a mako is always aware of its surroundings. They also have ampullae of Lorenzini. All these senses help mako sharks find creatures to eat.

BABIES

A mako shark normally travels alone. But eventually it needs to mate. A male shortfin mako shark is ready to reproduce by about age eight. It is believed that female shortfin mako sharks can reproduce around age 18. After mating, the female shark becomes pregnant.

Makos have white undersides.

Shortfin makos can live for around 30 years, if they are not caught by a sport fisher first.

Makos carry their eggs inside of them. In the early stages, the pups live off nutrition inside their eggs. Eventually this nutrition runs out, and they hatch. But the pups remain inside the mother's body. In order to survive, the baby sharks eat other unfertilized eggs.

The shortfin mako has an average litter size of 12. Shortfins are about 2 feet (0.6 m) long at birth. Longfin pups are believed to have two to eight pups in a litter. The pups are about 3.1 to 4 feet (0.9 to 1.2 m) long.

ATTACK AND DEFENSE

Mako sharks are deadly hunters. They have few natural predators. But makos must watch out for swordfish. This powerful fish uses its bill as a weapon. A swordfish can easily injure a mako shark.

Makos also fear humans. Adult makos are considered prized game fish. Many people like the challenge of

Shortfin makos could be dangerous to people.

fishing for mako sharks. The mako's fighting ability is its best defense against humans.

Catching a mako can be very dangerous. They do not like to be attacked. Angry makos have destroyed boats and hurt fishers.

Mako sharks are more than game fish. They are fished for their oil, fins, skins, jaws, and teeth. The fins are used in shark fin soup. A mako shark's skin is used for leather. And its jaws and teeth become souvenirs.

People catch and kill mako sharks.

SHARK FACTS

Nurse sharks are quite lazy. They spend their days resting on the ocean's bottom. Nurse sharks sometimes rest in groups of up to 40 individuals. Often, they pile on top of

In some areas, such as Brazil, the nurse shark is considered a vulnerable species.

each other. But don't let these sleepy sharks fool you. At night, nurse sharks become fierce hunters.

There are three nurse shark species. These are the short-tail nurse shark, the nurse shark, and the tawny nurse shark. Little is known about the secretive short-tail nurse shark. Scientists are working hard to study and gain more information about these creatures.

WHAT THEY LOOK LIKE

Nurse sharks have thick bodies and wide heads. Their skin is covered in tooth-like scales called denticles. These scales provide protection for the skin.

The short-tail nurse shark is the smallest nurse shark species. It grows to just 2.5 feet (0.8 m) long. This shark is dark brown.

On average, the female nurse shark is 7 to 9 feet (2.1 to 2.7 m) long. Some people say that this shark can grow up to 14 feet (4.3 m). The nurse shark's caudal fin can make up one-fourth of its total length. Most adult nurse sharks weigh

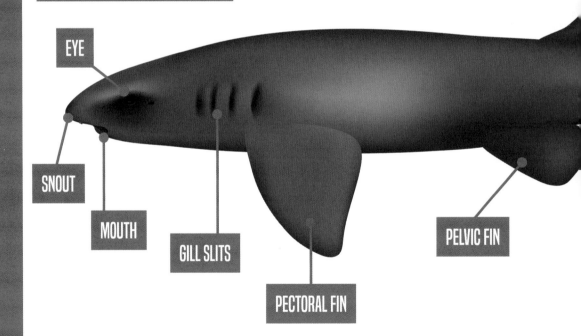

SHORT-TAIL NURSE SHARK

EYE

SNOUT

MOUTH

GILL SLITS

PECTORAL FIN

PELVIC FIN

DORSAL FINS

ANAL FIN

CAUDAL FIN

between 160 and 270 pounds (70 and 120 kg). They range from light yellowish tan to dark brown.

Tawny nurse sharks can be up to 10 feet (3 m) in length. These sharks are gray brown or brown in color.

WHERE THEY LIVE

Nurse sharks prefer warm water. They occupy tropical and subtropical oceans. The short-tail nurse shark lives in the western Indian Ocean. This shark spends its time near islands and continental shelves.

Nurse sharks live close to shore in the Atlantic and eastern Pacific Oceans. During the day, they rest along reefs and rocky areas. The water there is 10 to 250 feet (3 to 75 m) deep. These sharks move to shallower water at night to hunt.

WHERE DO NURSE SHARKS LIVE?

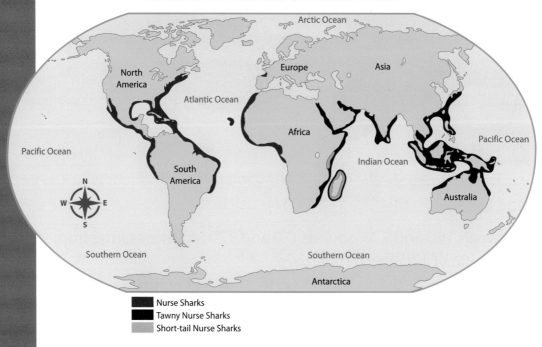

Nurse Sharks
Tawny Nurse Sharks
Short-tail Nurse Sharks

Tawny nurse sharks swim in the Indian and western Pacific Oceans. There, they live in coral reefs and lagoons. These sleepy sharks even occupy sandy surf areas. They are most common in water that is 16 to 98 feet (5 to 30 m) deep.

FOOD

Nurse sharks are not fast swimmers. So, they prey on resting creatures. These nocturnal sharks love eating fish. They also feed on crustaceans. Other prey includes mollusks such as octopuses, squid, and clams.

Tawny nurse sharks eat a variety of creatures. These include sea urchins and crustaceans. They also feed on small fish such

Nurse sharks have been known to eat stingrays.

as surgeonfish, queenfish, and rabbitfish. Sometimes they even eat sea snakes. Short-tail nurse sharks feed on things such as mollusks, fish, and shrimp.

When hunting, nurse sharks swim slowly over the ocean floor. If they detect hidden prey, they suck it right out of its hiding hole.

A nurse shark scans the ocean floor, looking for food.

SENSES

The nurse shark species uses its five senses to catch prey: sight, taste, smell, touch, and hearing. They also have other senses to locate prey and mates. Like other sharks, nurse sharks have a sensitive lateral line system. Also, using special sense organs in their heads, sharks can detect electric fields. This sense is another way nurse sharks find their next meals.

The nurse shark's scientific name means "curled, hinged mouth."

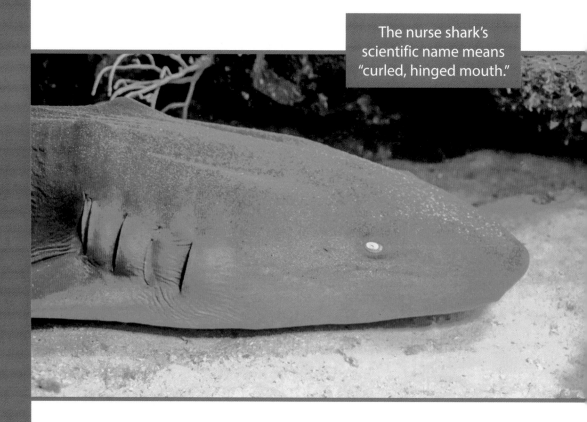

Sharks will sometimes fight over food.

BABIES

Nurse shark pups hatch from eggs inside the mother and are born live. At birth, the pups have teeth. They also have dark spots on the skin. These spots fade as the sharks age. The pups are able to swim and hunt right away.

The tawny nurse shark is an active species.

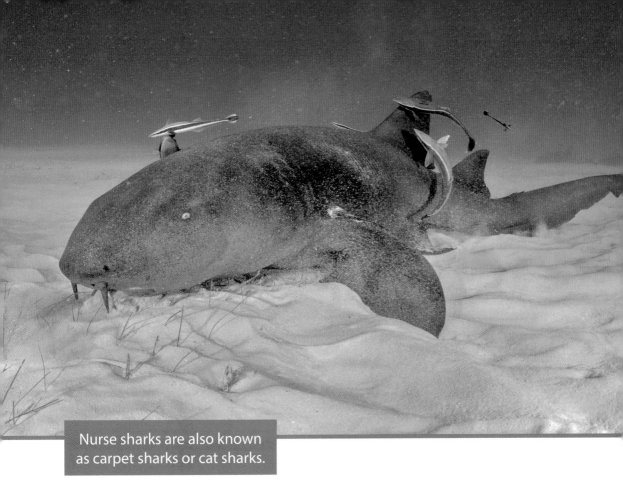

Nurse sharks are also known as carpet sharks or cat sharks.

A female nurse shark is pregnant for about six months. She can have around 20 to 40 pups at a time. The pups are about 12 inches (30 cm) long at birth.

Tawny nurse shark mothers have up to eight pups. When they are born, the pups are about 15 to 24 inches (38 to 61 cm) long.

ATTACK AND DEFENSE

Nurse sharks have small mouths and simple teeth. The teeth are made for crushing and gripping rather than for cutting. But nurse sharks have powerful jaws and a strong bite. This makes them fearsome predators.

A nurse shark catches a stingray.

Nurse sharks don't have many predators, but they can still get injured by other sharks.

In addition, nurse sharks hunt at night. This allows them to catch resting prey that might normally be too speedy for these sharks.

A large nurse shark has almost nothing to fear except humans. No predators regularly hunt these sharks. Occasionally, a nurse shark becomes a larger shark's meal. These larger sharks include lemon, tiger, bull, and hammerhead sharks. Nurse sharks defend themselves by blending into the ocean's bottom.

SAND SHARKS *(CARCHARIAS TAURUS)*

SHARK FACTS

The sand shark is large and has a snaggletoothed look. This bulky shark is known by many different names. These include gray nurse shark, spotted ragged-tooth shark, and sand tiger shark.

Some scientists think sand sharks can live between 30 to 35 years.

Some aquariums have sand sharks.

Even though they look vicious with their many teeth, sand sharks are not known to be aggressive. These sharks reproduce slowly, so people try to protect this species. They don't want it to become endangered.

WHAT THEY LOOK LIKE

The sand shark has a thick body and a flattened, cone-shaped snout. There are five gill slits on either side of its head. The shark's caudal fin is longer than it is broad. Its upper lobe is larger than the lower lobe.

Besides the caudal fin, a sand shark has four other kinds of fins. Two dorsal fins, two pelvic fins, and one anal fin keep the shark stable. The shark uses its two pectoral fins to steer.

Pointy teeth fill the sand shark's long mouth. The teeth stick out in all directions. You can see them even when the mouth is closed.

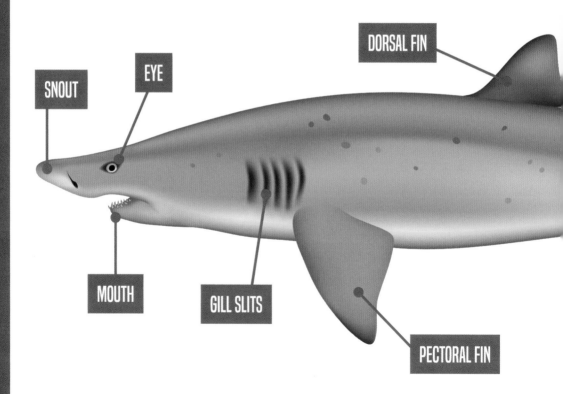

SNOUT

EYE

DORSAL FIN

MOUTH

GILL SLITS

PECTORAL FIN

These fierce-looking sharks are light brown or light greenish in color. They have rusty or brown spots. Their bellies are whitish.

Sand sharks are usually 4 to 9 feet (1 to 3 m) long, but these sharks can grow bigger. The largest sand shark on record was around 10.5 feet (3.2 m) long.

Sand sharks have ferocious-looking teeth.

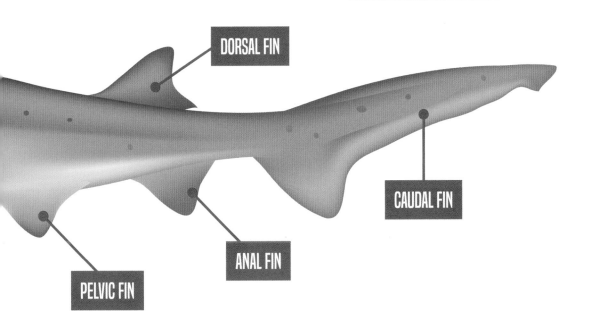

DORSAL FIN

CAUDAL FIN

ANAL FIN

PELVIC FIN

WHERE THEY LIVE

Sand sharks occupy most temperate and tropical ocean waters. However, they do not live in the eastern Pacific Ocean.

This shark received its name because it is common in shallow water near shore. But sand sharks also venture offshore. They can be seen along the ocean bottom. They can also be found at middle depths and at the surface.

WHERE DO SAND SHARKS LIVE?

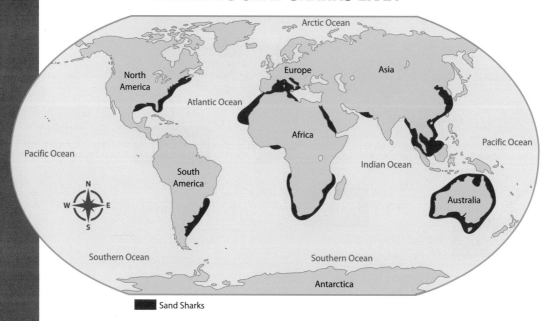

Sand Sharks

Sand sharks prefer to remain near the ocean floor.

These sharks migrate seasonally. In summer, they move toward the poles to cool off. They head for warmer water near the equator in fall and winter.

FOOD

Sand sharks hunt at night, staying close to the ocean floor. These large fish have big appetites. They eat a wide variety of bony fish. These include herring, eels, bonitos, and snappers. They also feed on squid, crabs, lobsters, and smaller sharks.

Herring are also food for tuna, salmon, and even humans.

A sand shark's teeth help it slice into prey.

Sand sharks usually swim alone. However, they have been observed hunting in schools. Together, the sharks chase prey into a tight group. Then, they feed on the trapped fish. Even with all their teeth, sand sharks swallow their prey whole.

SENSES

Visibility can be poor in seawater. To find prey in these conditions, sand sharks rely on their other senses. Sounds, vibrations, and scents travel well through water. Sharks are very sensitive to these things.

The sand shark belongs to the family *Odontaspididae*.

Sharks have many senses that help them function well underwater.

Sand sharks use their ears to hear. They also use their lateral line systems to detect sounds and vibrations. Like other sharks, sand sharks can sense electric fields. Sensing electric fields helps sand sharks navigate and find hidden prey.

BABIES

Sand sharks begin life as eggs inside the mother. There, the babies hatch and continue to develop. As they grow, the babies feed on unhatched eggs. They also eat their siblings. Just two pups will survive this period of development.

A female sand shark gives birth about once every two years.

Some sand sharks have spots.

In eight to nine months, the female shark gives birth to her young. The pups are a little more than 3 feet (1 m) long. They each weigh about 13 pounds (6 kg). The pups are fully developed. They can swim and eat prey right away.

After delivering her pups, the mother swims away. The newborn sharks are left on their own to try to survive.

ATTACK AND DEFENSE

Like other sharks, sand sharks are heavier than water. They will sink if they stop swimming. Sand sharks are the only sharks known to surface to swallow air. The sharks then hold the air in their stomachs. This allows them to float and hover motionless over the ocean floor when hunting.

Divers should be respectful around any type of shark, even if the shark species is not as aggressive as others.

Many people are fascinated with sharks and want to learn more about them.

Sand sharks have pointy teeth suitable for catching and piercing prey. The upper jaw holds 44 to 48 teeth. There are 41 to 46 teeth in the lower jaw.

As adults, these fierce-looking sharks have no major predators. Larger sharks prey on pups and other young sand sharks. The young sharks must use their well-developed senses to avoid capture.

SHARK FACTS

A seal shark cruises through the water to look for its next meal. It may come across an animal much bigger than itself. Normally, a creature would pass by without thinking of attacking the larger animal. But, the seal shark has a unique way of feasting on the largest creatures of the sea.

Seal sharks are solitary animals. They rarely travel in schools.

The seal shark is also sometimes called the kitefin shark.

The seal shark is a fascinating animal. It lives deep in the ocean. The more scientists study these fish, the more information they learn.

117

WHAT THEY LOOK LIKE

Female seal sharks are larger than males. Adult females can grow to 3.8 to 5.2 feet (1.2 to 1.6 m) long. Males are around 2.5 to 4 feet (0.8 to 1.2 m) long.

Seal sharks have slender trunks and short, blunt snouts. They have large, pale lips. Their upper teeth are slender and curve outward toward the corners of the mouth. Their lower teeth are straight and triangular.

Seal sharks are a gray or dark brown color. Sometimes their backs are covered with black spots. The tail is capped with black. The dorsal and pectoral fins have whitish edges.

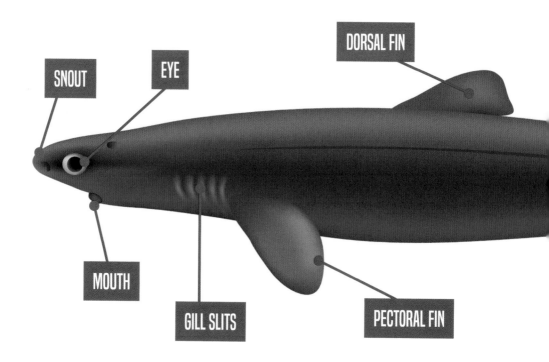

DORSAL FIN

SNOUT

EYE

MOUTH

GILL SLITS

PECTORAL FIN

Seal sharks have large eyes.

A seal shark's body is made for ocean living. Its liver is about 25 percent of its body weight. The liver contains oil that makes the shark float naturally in the water. And the seal shark's cartilaginous skeleton is lighter than bone.

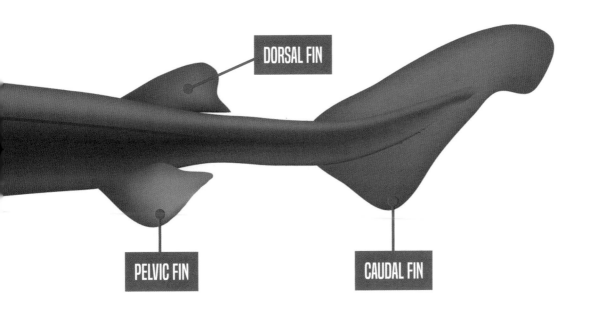

DORSAL FIN

PELVIC FIN

CAUDAL FIN

WHERE THEY LIVE

Seal sharks live near New Zealand, Australia, Japan, and the Hawaiian Islands. They swim through waters near the west coast of Africa up through Ireland. And they live in the northern Gulf of Mexico as well as in the western areas of the Mediterranean Sea.

Seal sharks are deepwater fish. Typically they are found between 656 to 1,970 feet (200 to 600 m) deep. But some have also been seen at 5,900 feet (1,800 m) deep. They are considered a bottom-dwelling species. But they often live far above the ocean floor.

WHERE DO SEAL SHARKS LIVE?

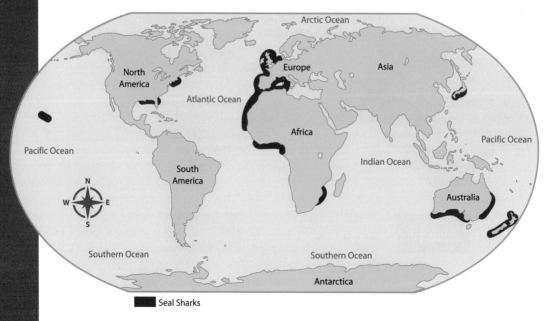

Seal Sharks

A variety of animals swim through Australia's waters.

Most sharks are cold blooded, including seal sharks. This means their body temperatures depend on the surrounding water. So sharks try to remain in places where they can maintain their body temperatures and feel comfortable. The seal shark chooses warm or tropical water to live in.

FOOD

There is plenty to eat in the ocean's deeper areas. Seal sharks feast on crustaceans, squid, octopuses, and annelid worms. They also eat a variety of bony fish and even some sharks.

There are thousands of annelid worm species.

This dolphin was the victim of a cookie-cutter shark attack. This bite is similar to the damage a seal shark would do. The cookie-cutter shark and seal shark are in the same family.

Larger creatures are not safe from the seal shark. With its tiny upper teeth, a seal shark hooks onto its target's body. The seal shark's large lips are used to suction, or attach, itself to the animal.

Once attached, the seal shark spins around in a circle. The lower rigid teeth cut a ball-like piece of flesh from the larger creature. This unusual feeding method leaves the seal shark's prey alive but scarred.

SENSES

Deep underwater, a seal shark has to figure out what is above, below, and near it. Seal sharks hear low vibrations, detect particles in the water—such as blood—through their noses, and sense electrical charges and changes in water pressure.

People send robots deep underwater to explore the ocean.

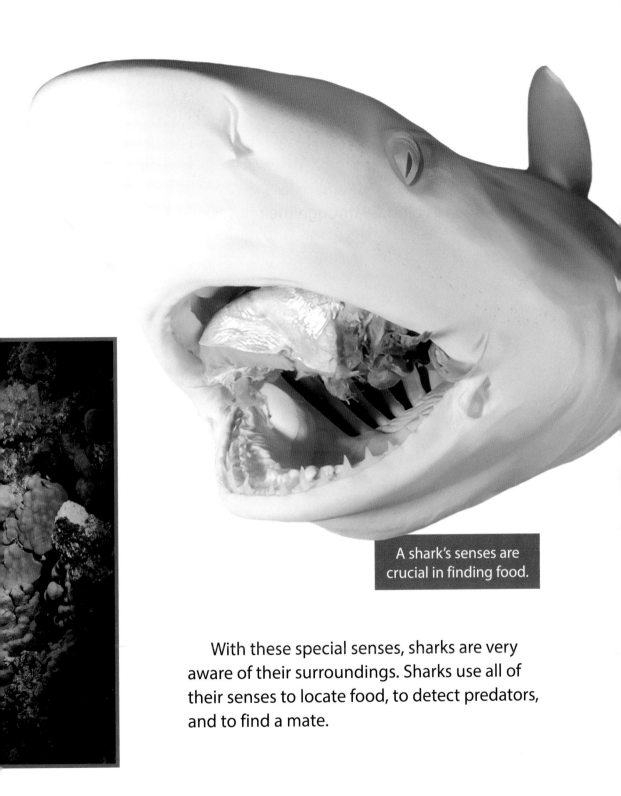

A shark's senses are crucial in finding food.

With these special senses, sharks are very aware of their surroundings. Sharks use all of their senses to locate food, to detect predators, and to find a mate.

BABIES

Reproduction is important to the survival of shark species. It takes a long time for sharks to reach maturity. So, it is important for them to live long enough to reproduce.

Scientists are not sure at what age seal sharks become mature. Male seal sharks are ready to reproduce when they are between 32 and 47 inches (80 and 120 cm) long. Female seal

Shark fishing is harmful to shark populations. If sharks cannot reproduce, the populations will not survive.

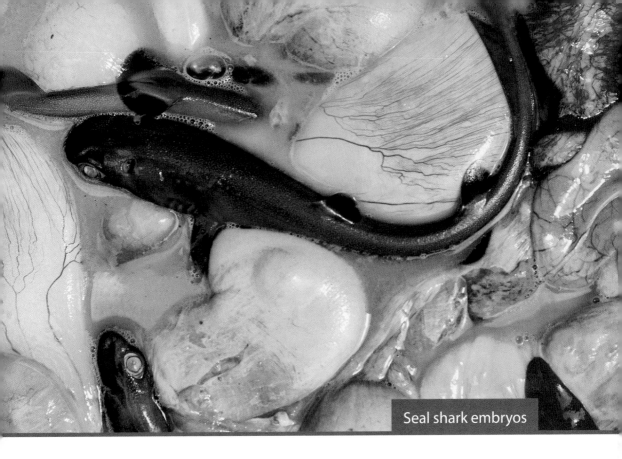

Seal shark embryos

sharks are mature when they reach 47 to 55 inches (120 to 140 cm) in length.

After an adult male and female mate, the baby sharks begin to develop. Seal sharks grow in eggs inside their mothers. A yolk sac is attached to each embryo. This provides the nourishment the developing sharks need.

Seal shark pups are birthed in litters of ten to 16 young. They are typically around 12 inches (30 cm) long at birth. Seal shark pups are born fully developed and ready for the world. Still, the pups will have to be clever to survive. The mother swims away soon after her babies are born.

ATTACK AND DEFENSE

The seal shark is a powerful predator. Seal sharks attack creatures much larger than themselves. Using their teeth, they take perfect round plugs out of their victims. But a seal shark has no defense against humans. The seal shark's biggest threat is commercial fishing. Increases in deepwater fishing have reduced the seal shark's numbers. This has made the seal shark a vulnerable species.

Sometimes a seal shark's skin is made into leather.

Overfishing can hurt fish populations, including those of sharks.

SHARK FACTS

There are three species of thresher sharks: the thresher, the bigeye thresher, and the pelagic thresher. Each species has the large tail typical of a thresher shark. They are strong, active swimmers. They are most often found near the surface of the water.

Thresher sharks have noticeably long tails.

Sharks are carnivores—they eat meat. Most sharks eat live fish.

Thresher sharks are not aggressive creatures. They prefer to shy away from people. So, they are not considered harmful. However, because of their large sizes and their strong tails, thresher sharks should be avoided.

WHAT THEY LOOK LIKE

Thresher sharks have a short, pointed snout and a short head. They have long, narrow pectoral fins and a large front dorsal fin. Their small teeth are blade-like.

Thresher sharks have dark backs and light bellies. The color on their backs blends into spots on their undersides near the tail. This color pattern helps hide these sharks in the water.

Female thresher sharks can grow to be around 8.5 to 15 feet (2.6 to 4.5 m) long. Males can be around 10.5 feet (3.2 m) long. But thresher sharks grow about 4 inches (10 cm) every year. One thresher shark reached almost 25 feet (7.6 m) long. The average bigeye thresher is around 11 to 13 feet (3.4 to 4 m). And the pelagic thresher only reaches a maximum size of about 10 feet (3 m).

The most obvious way to identify a thresher shark is by its giant tail. The tail of the thresher makes up about one-half of its body length. Thresher sharks use their powerful tails in combination with their large front fins for swimming. They also use their tails for hunting.

CAUDAL FIN

Thresher sharks will whip their tails against prey.

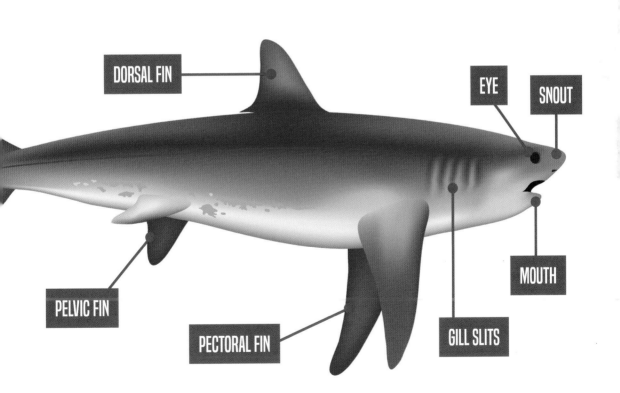

DORSAL FIN

EYE

SNOUT

PELVIC FIN

PECTORAL FIN

GILL SLITS

MOUTH

WHERE THEY LIVE

Thresher sharks live throughout the world's oceans. They occupy temperate to tropical regions of the Atlantic, Pacific, and Indian Oceans. They are most often found close to shore. But they can also be found very far out to sea.

Young thresher sharks often travel into bays. Adult thresher sharks are common over the continental shelf. Thresher sharks can be found up to 1,200 feet (370 m) below the surface. Bigeye threshers have been found as deep as 1,640 feet (500 m).

WHERE DO THRESHER SHARKS LIVE?

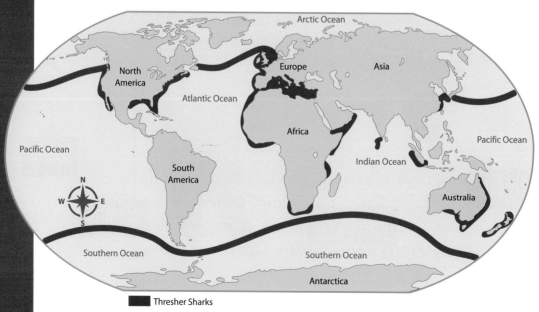

■ Thresher Sharks

Thresher sharks are known to leap out of the water. It takes a very powerful creature to jump completely out of the water. This is even more amazing because of the thresher shark's massive size.

Throughout the year, thresher sharks migrate many miles. During the summer months, thresher sharks can be found far from the equator. Water temperatures are warm enough for them to live as far north as Norway. During the winter, they return to waters near the equator.

FOOD

In nature, animals use their natural abilities for survival. A thresher shark's greatest gift for survival is its tail. Thresher sharks hunt schools of fish by swimming in circles around them.

When hunting, the thresher shark uses its tail to herd the fish together. Then, the shark slaps its tail. That slapping action stuns some of the fish in the school. The shark feeds on the stunned fish. It is an effective way for a creature to use its natural abilities to capture a meal.

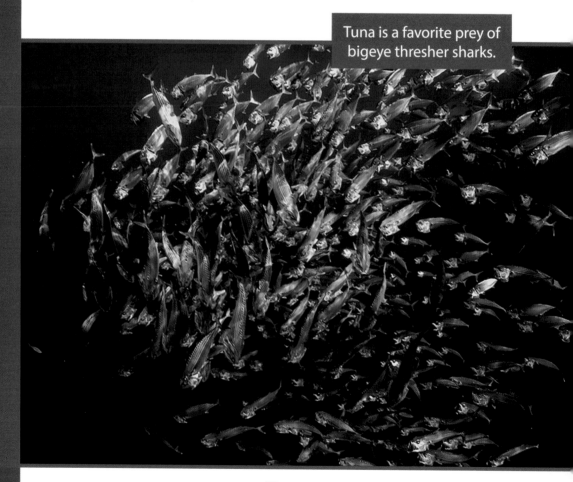

Tuna is a favorite prey of bigeye thresher sharks.

An octopus can be a meal for thresher sharks.

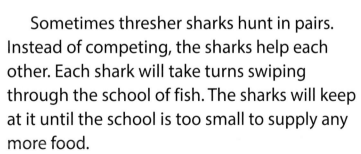

Sometimes thresher sharks hunt in pairs. Instead of competing, the sharks help each other. Each shark will take turns swiping through the school of fish. The sharks will keep at it until the school is too small to supply any more food.

The main sources of food for thresher sharks are these schools of fish. Other times, a meal has to come from a wider variety of creatures. Thresher sharks also feed on squid and octopuses.

SENSES

Thresher sharks have well-developed eyes. They have a strong sense of smell that works underwater. And they have a keen sense of hearing that helps them find prey.

Thresher sharks can sense vibrations with their lateral line systems. They can also sense electrical charges with their ampullae of Lorenzini.

Thresher sharks have the ability to detect pressure changes in the water. Pressure changes tell them the water depth. By using all of their senses, these sharks can understand their surroundings and find the food they need.

Some sharks have good eyesight to help them navigate underwater.

Bigeye threshers are named for their enormous eyes.

BABIES

It takes around eight to 13 years for thresher sharks to become mature enough for mating. This is due to the slow growth rate of many large shark species.

The eggs remain inside the mother after they are fertilized. As they develop, each embryo lives off the nourishment inside its egg. Eventually the yolk in the egg runs out. Then, the embryos have to find another source for food. Throughout the pregnancy, the mother shark continues to release eggs. The embryos eat these eggs as well as smaller embryos in order to survive.

The size of thresher shark pups at birth depends on how big the mother is.

Thresher sharks can sometimes be seen at the water's surface.

Mother thresher sharks birth two to four young at a time. These pups are well developed and ready for life. Baby sharks do not remain near their mothers. The mother swims away soon after her pups are born.

Bigeye threshers are about 3 to 4.5 feet (1 to 1.4 m) long at birth. The pelagic thresher is between 5 and 6 feet (1.5 to 1.8 m) long. Thresher shark pups can be around 3.7 to 5 feet (1 to 1.5 m) long.

ATTACK AND DEFENSE

Thresher sharks use body coloring as a form of defense. Their bodies blend into the water whether viewed from above or below. Being hidden helps these sharks sneak up on prey and hide from predators.

Larger sharks prey on young thresher sharks. But adult thresher sharks have no natural predators. Their biggest threat

Some divers who have gone near thresher sharks say that the sharks did not show signs of aggression.

People catch and kill thresher sharks.

is humans. The thresher shark's long tail often gets them hooked by fishers.

Thresher sharks are hunted commercially and for sport. Their meat is used for food, and their skins are used for leather. A shark's liver is a source of vitamins and oil. In some cultures, shark fin soup is a popular meal.

Thresher sharks also battle parasites. Parasites attach to the thresher shark's gill filaments and can cause damage. This damage can lead to breathing problems.

SHARK FACTS

Tiger sharks are usually slow swimmers. But they will move fast to catch prey. This species is known for its interesting diet. Tiger sharks will try to eat anything, including people. The tiger

Tiger sharks are one of the largest shark species. Some have been recorded as long as 18 feet (5.5 m).

shark is one of the most dangerous sharks to humans. Only the great white shark has been involved in more attacks on people. Tiger sharks don't hunt humans. Yet, they are curious when they encounter divers and swimmers. And they can be aggressive. Humans should always respect these fierce sharks.

Tiger sharks sometimes travel in groups.

WHAT THEY LOOK LIKE

The tiger shark's name comes from the tiger-like stripes and spots on its skin. These markings fade as the shark ages. The tiger shark is bluish green to dark gray or black on top. Its belly is yellowish white to white.

The tiger shark has a robust head. It features two large eyes and five gill slits on each side of the head. The blunt snout contains a wide mouth armed with sharp, serrated teeth.

Every tiger shark has five kinds of fins. The dorsal, anal, and pelvic fins help keep the shark stable when swimming. The pectoral fins are for steering. And the caudal fin moves the shark forward.

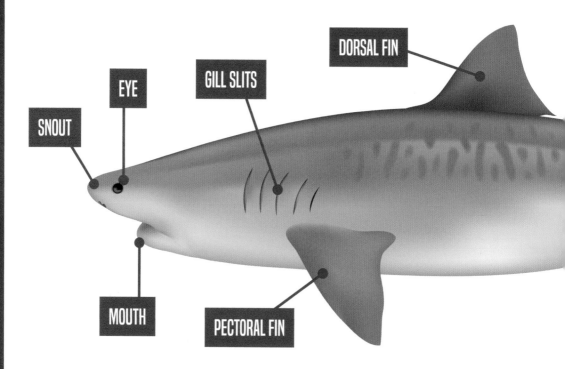

SNOUT

EYE

GILL SLITS

DORSAL FIN

MOUTH

PECTORAL FIN

As tiger sharks get older, their stripes will fade.

Full-grown tiger sharks are large fish. They reach lengths of 10 to 14 feet (3 to 4 m). And they weigh 850 to 1,400 pounds (390 to 640 kg).

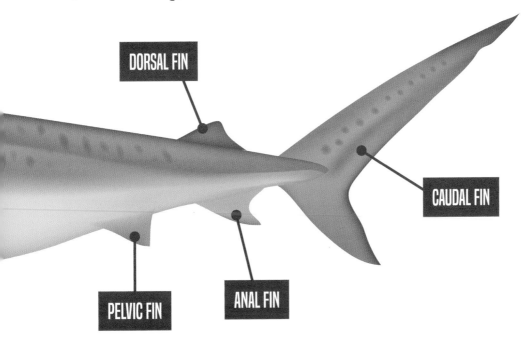

DORSAL FIN

CAUDAL FIN

PELVIC FIN

ANAL FIN

WHERE THEY LIVE

Tiger sharks are found worldwide. They live in all temperate and tropical waters. Tiger sharks are often seen close to the water's surface. However, they may also dive as deep as 1,150 feet (350 m).

These fierce sharks prefer to live in murky coastal waters. They are common in lagoons, harbors, and where river currents meet the ocean's tide. Tiger sharks have also been spotted far offshore.

As the seasons change, tiger sharks migrate. During warmer months, they move from tropical to temperate waters. They return to warm waters in winter.

WHERE DO TIGER SHARKS LIVE?

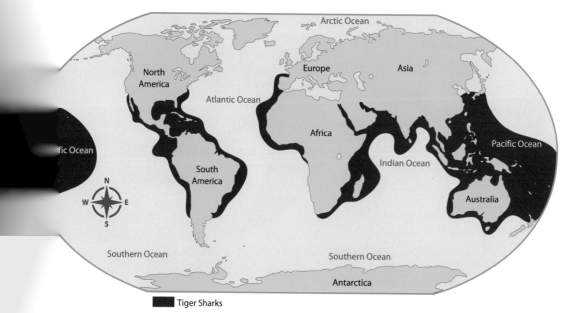

Tiger Sharks

The tiger shark belongs to the family *Carcharhinidae*.

FOOD

Tiger sharks like to feed at night. They often hunt alone. Sometimes they form loose schools when there is a large amount of food around.

These sharks eat bony fish, rays, sea snakes, dolphins, seabirds, and other sharks. They also eat armored prey such as sea turtles. But tiger

Tiger sharks will eat green sea turtles.

A tiger shark's sharp teeth make it easy to rip into prey.

sharks are really known for the junk they consume. A variety of human items have been found in their stomachs. These include tin cans, clothing, plastic bottles, and burlap sacks. None of these are good for tiger sharks.

SENSES

The tiger shark's many well-developed senses make it a dangerous predator. Its large eyes see well in dim water. This amazing creature also has a good sense of smell. If prey is injured or bleeding, a tiger shark can locate it from a long distance.

Tiger sharks are also called leopard sharks, spotted sharks, and maneater sharks.

Tiger sharks can move fast when they sense something tasty.

Like all sharks, the tiger shark senses the weak electric fields all living animals give off. This sense may lead a tiger shark to its next meal. It also helps the shark navigate.

In addition, sharks have excellent hearing. They use their ears and lateral line systems to detect sounds and vibrations. Using these sensitive systems tells sharks about their surroundings.

BABIES

A baby tiger shark begins life inside its mother as an egg. Instead of laying her eggs, the mother shark carries them inside her. There, the eggs hatch after 13 to 16 months. Soon after, the baby sharks are born live. A mother tiger shark gives birth to ten to 82 pups.

Tiger shark pups can be 20 to 30 inches (50 to 75 cm) long at birth. Once they are born, the pups are on their own. Luckily, they are fully developed and able to swim.

Juvenile tiger sharks have clear markings.

Tiger sharks in the northern hemisphere will mate between March and May.

Newborn tiger sharks have many predators to fear. Even larger tiger sharks will eat them. The young sharks use their strong senses to hunt and survive.

ATTACK AND DEFENSE

A tiger shark's teeth are its greatest weapons. They are made to snag and cut prey. There is not much these sharp teeth can't saw into.

Shark teeth grow in rows. When a tooth breaks or falls out, a new one replaces it. The dangerous tiger shark's large mouth

Tiger sharks can be aggressive. Only trained professionals should get close.

Tiger sharks are curious creatures. Sometimes trained divers will feed sharks to get near them.

is filled with teeth. There are about 24 teeth in every row.

Size and fierceness are a tiger shark's greatest defenses. An adult tiger shark has little to fear except man. Fishers are eager to catch these sharks for their fins, flesh, and skins. Tiger sharks are also caught for sport.

SHARK FACTS

Sharks come in all shapes and sizes. The whale shark is the biggest shark species and the world's largest fish. This slow-moving giant is one of three large filter-feeder sharks. These sharks use their gills to strain food from ocean water.

Whale sharks are little threat to humans. Sometimes divers approach these gentle sharks and even ride them. Whale sharks

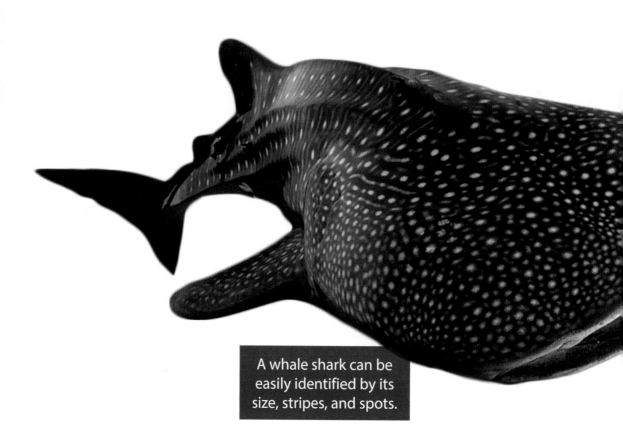

A whale shark can be easily identified by its size, stripes, and spots.

These sharks can open
their mouths very wide.

are curious about people, too. They may swim
near people to check them out.

Human interaction with these giants is not
always gentle. Whale sharks have bumped
into boats. And boaters have run into these
giant fish.

WHAT THEY LOOK LIKE

Whale sharks are huge fish. They are capable of growing nearly 60 feet (18 m) long. Most whale sharks are 39 feet (12 m) long and weigh about 15 tons (14 t).

The whale shark has a wide, flattened head and large gill slits. Its mouth is nearly at the end of its snout. It has hundreds of rows of tiny teeth that fill its huge mouth. Yet, this shark does not use its teeth for feeding.

This long, thick shark displays a unique color pattern. Its back is grayish, bluish, or brownish. Light spots and stripes form a checkerboard pattern on this dark background. The whale shark's belly is white.

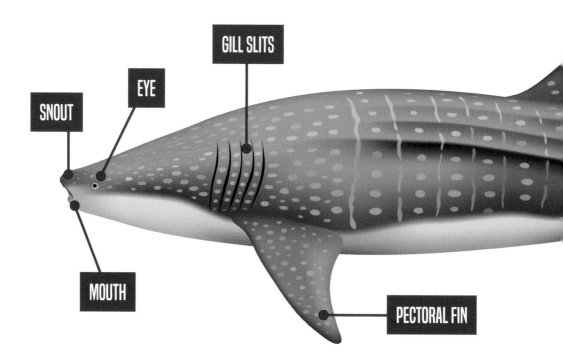

GILL SLITS

EYE

SNOUT

MOUTH

PECTORAL FIN

Whale sharks are the only members of the family *Rhincodontidae*.

The whale shark's fins keep this large shark stable and allow it to steer. The large caudal fin moves the shark through the water.

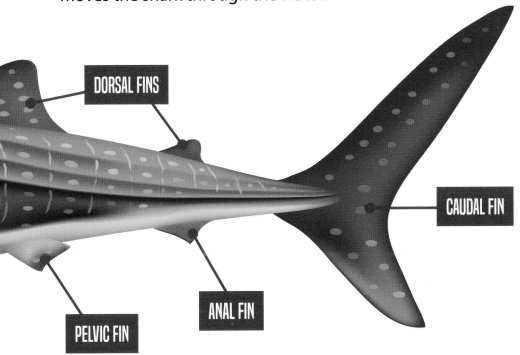

DORSAL FINS

CAUDAL FIN

ANAL FIN

PELVIC FIN

WHERE THEY LIVE

Whale sharks like warm ocean water. They live in almost all tropical and warm temperate seas. But they do not occupy the Mediterranean Sea.

Whale sharks live throughout the Indian Ocean. In the Atlantic Ocean, these sharks range from New York to central Brazil. They are also found from Senegal in Africa to the Gulf of Guinea.

In the Pacific Ocean, whale sharks range from Japan to Australia. They also live off Hawaii's coasts and from California to Chile.

WHERE DO WHALE SHARKS LIVE?

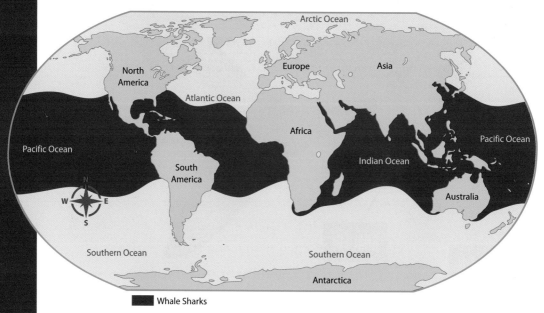

■ Whale Sharks

Researchers believe whale sharks migrate seasonally. They may do this for food.

These gentle giants swim near the water's surface. They are often spotted far offshore. But they also travel inshore. Whale sharks are usually found alone.

FOOD

Whale sharks feed at or near the water's surface. As filter feeders, these giant sharks feast on a variety of plankton. Whale sharks also eat mollusks. And they feed on fish, such as sardines, mackerel, and tuna.

Whale sharks suck up food with their mouths.

Whale sharks will shift their large heads from side to side to get food.

Sometimes the whale shark feeds in a vertical position, with its head pointed toward the surface. As the shark bobs up and down, food enters its mouth.

However, this shark usually feeds while cruising through the water. It opens its mouth and sucks in food and water. This action works much like a vacuum cleaner.

When its huge mouth is full, the whale shark closes its jaws. This traps prey and water inside. To get to its food, the shark forces the water out through its gills. The gills act like strainers, filtering food from the water. The whale shark swallows anything retained in its mouth.

SENSES

As the largest fish in the world, whale sharks must find lots of food. Their senses of smell play a large role in hunting. Their senses of taste are well developed, too.

Whale sharks have small eyes that are located far back on their heads. So, researchers do not believe eyesight helps whale sharks hunt.

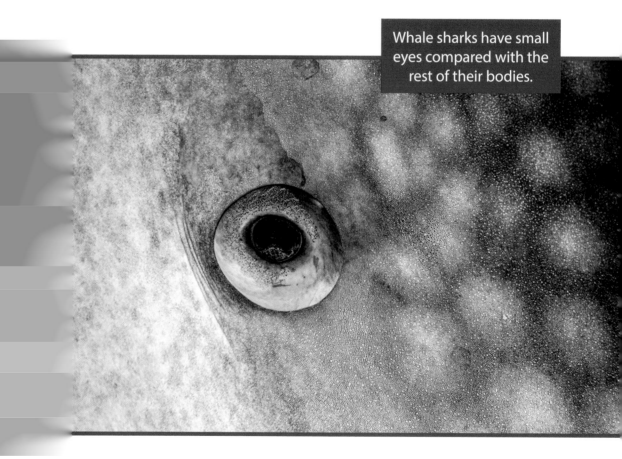

Whale sharks have small eyes compared with the rest of their bodies.

A whale shark's senses are important to helping it survive.

All sharks use sense organs in their heads to detect electric fields. Also, whale sharks have lateral line systems. This can lead the shark to its next meal or warn it of danger.

BABIES

Researchers know little about whale shark reproduction. Most of their information is from a female whale shark captured in 1995. She was carrying 300 baby sharks inside her. The babies were 17 to 25 inches (42 to 63 cm) long.

The whale shark's large mouth is perfectly suited to filter feeding. It is not made to grab large prey.

There is still much to learn about whale shark reproduction.

This discovery told researchers that whale shark mothers do not lay their eggs. The eggs hatch inside the mother, and the babies continue to develop there. Eventually, the mother gives birth to live young. Researchers believe the pups measure 21 to 25 inches (53 to 63.5 cm) long at birth. It is not yet known how many pups are born in a litter.

ATTACK AND DEFENSE

The whale shark does not have to worry much about predators. Few animals would even attempt to take on this large creature.

However, these sharks are not so big at birth. So, young whale sharks have a little more to fear than adults. They have been found in the stomachs of other shark species.

Whale sharks have been known to get close to divers.

Whale sharks can be seen at the ocean's surface.

The whale shark's skin may play a role in its defense. It is up to 6 inches (15 cm) thick. Not much can easily cut through it. Yet, parasites may attach themselves to the shark's skin. Whale sharks often rub against boats to remove these unwelcome guests.

BLACKTIP REEF SHARK

Scientific name: *Carcharhinus melanopterus*
Size: 5 feet (1.5 m) long; around 286 pounds (130 kg)
Where They're Found: Around places such as Australia, China, Japan, India, Madagascar, and the Philippines

BLUE SHARK

Scientific name: *Prionace glauca*
Size: 6.5 to 9.8 feet (2 to 3 m) long; 205 to 400 pounds (93 to 182 kg) for females and 60 to 120 pounds (27 to 55 kg) for males
Where They're Found: Cold ocean waters around the world

BROWNBANDED BAMBOO SHARK

Scientific name: *Chiloscyllium punctatum*

Size: Can reach 3.5 feet (1 m) long

Where They're Found: Around areas such as Thailand, India, Singapore, Malaysia, Indonesia, China, Vietnam, Japan, Taiwan, the Philippines, Australia, and New Guinea

CHAIN CATSHARK *(ALSO KNOWN AS CHAIN DOGFISH)*

Scientific name: *Scyliorhinus retifer*

Size: 1.3 feet (0.4 m) long; can be around 1.5 pounds (0.7 kg)

Where They're Found: From Massachusetts to Nicaragua

DUSKY SHARK

Scientific name: *Carcharhinus obscurus*
Size: Can be more than 11 feet (3.3 m) long and can reach 400 pounds (180 kg)
Where They're Found: Temperate and tropical waters from Nova Scotia to Cuba, Nicaragua to Brazil, California, the Mediterranean, and around Australia and Madagascar

GOBLIN SHARK

Scientific name: *Mitsukurina owstoni*
Size: 10 to 13 feet (3 to 4 m) long
Where They're Found: Atlantic and Indian Oceans and the western Pacific

GREENLAND SHARK

Scientific name: *Somniosus microcephalus*
Size: 8 to 14 feet (2.4 to 4.3 m) long
Where They're Found: Arctic and North Atlantic Oceans

HORN SHARK

Scientific name: *Heterodontus francisci*
Size: 3.2 feet (1 m) long; can be around
22 pounds (10 kg)
Where They're Found: Between central
California and the Gulf of California

LEOPARD CATSHARK

Scientific name: *Poroderma pantherinum*
Size: Can be around 2.5 feet (0.8 m) long
Where They're Found: Southeast
Atlantic Ocean

MEGAMOUTH SHARK

Scientific name: *Megachasma pelagios*
Size: 17 feet (5 m) long
Where They're Found: Atlantic, Indian, and
Pacific Oceans

PORT JACKSON SHARK

Scientific name: *Heterodontus portusjacksoni*
Size: 4.5 feet (1.4 m) long
Where They're Found: The coast of southern Australia

SILVERTIP SHARK

Scientific name: *Carcharhinus albimarginatus*
Size: 6.6 to 8.2 feet (2 to 2.5 m) long; can reach 358 pounds (162 kg)
Where They're Found: Western Indian Ocean, western Pacific, and east central Pacific

TASSELLED WOBBEGONG

Scientific name: *Eucrossorhinus dasypogon*
Size: 4 feet (1.2 m) long
Where They're Found: Northern Australia, eastern Indonesia, and Papua New Guinea

WHITETIP REEF SHARK

Scientific name: *Triaenodon obesus*
Size: 5.3 feet (1.6 m) long; can weigh up to 40 pounds (18 kg)
Where They're Found: Pacific Ocean and Indian Ocean

SHARK ATTACK

People need to be careful when swimming in areas with sharks.

One morning, 42-year-old Allan Oppert and two of his friends went to a familiar diving spot off the coast of western Australia. They strapped on their gear and spent the morning exploring the deep blue ocean. Oppert started his third dive of the day, and he was 55 feet (17 m) below the surface when a large great white shark appeared below him.

The shark hit him with such force that Oppert's face mask fell off and hung around his neck. He clenched his teeth around the mouthpiece where he was getting air. The shark's own teeth sunk into his legs. The great white shook Oppert back and forth and eventually let go, allowing Oppert to rise quickly to the surface. Oppert survived the attack.

Between 2013 and 2017, there was an average of 84 shark attacks every year. Around six people die each year from these attacks. In 2018, the United States experienced the most shark attacks, with 32 attacks leading to one death. Most of these attacks happened in Florida. Australia reported 20 attacks and one death. The next countries with the most attacks were Brazil and Egypt. Both of these countries reported three attacks each.

ACTIVITY OF VICTIMS WHEN ATTACKED

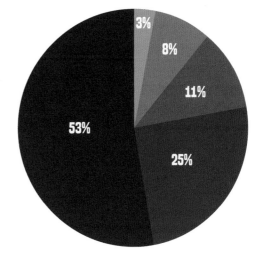

- ■ BOARD ACTIVITIES AND SURFING
- ■ WADING OR SWIMMING
- ■ FREE DIVING OR SNORKELING
- ■ ROUGHHOUSING OR BODY SURFING
- ■ SCUBA DIVING

It can be difficult for people to figure out which species of shark attacked them. In the heat of the moment, people can misidentify the shark. However, experts think that great white sharks, tiger sharks, and bull sharks are likely the top three involved in shark attacks. There are three reasons for this. First, these species are large and could seriously hurt people. Second, their teeth slice instead of hold their victims. Third, they live in waters that people also visit. When humans go into areas where sharks could be swimming, the chance of interactions between the two goes up.

Sometimes sharks mistake people for food. They will bite a human to see if they can eat him or her, and then they often leave. Sharks don't naturally prey on humans. And sometimes attacks happen because sharks are curious and are trying to figure out why a strange object—a human—is in the water. Experts say that when attacks happen, sharks don't show behaviors of their normal hunting techniques. This leads experts to believe that sharks aren't aiming to eat people. Another reason for shark attacks could be because of territory. If a shark has decided that a certain area is where it will be feeding, it doesn't want other sharks—or people—in the area.

Overall, more sharks die because of humans than the other way around. According to the Florida Museum of Natural History, people kill around 100 million rays and sharks every year. This has greatly hurt shark populations worldwide.

GLOSSARY

carnivore

An animal or plant that eats meat.

cartilage

The soft, elastic connective tissue in the skeleton. A person's nose and ears are made of cartilage.

continental shelf

A shallow, underwater plain forming a continent's border. It ends with a steep slope to the deep ocean floor.

crustacean

Any of a group of animals with hard shells that live mostly in water. Crabs, lobsters, and shrimps are all crustaceans.

dorsal

Located near or on the back, especially of an animal.

embryo

An organism in the early stages of development.

larva

The early form of an animal, such as a tadpole, that must change before it is in its adult form.

lobe

A rounded projecting part, as of a body part or a leaf.

migrate

To move from one place to another, often to find food.

odorant

A fragrant substance.

parasite

An organism that lives off of another organism of a different species.

pectoral

Located in or on the chest.

plankton

Small animals and plants that float in a body of water.

pore

A small opening in an animal or plant through which matter passes.

temperate

Having neither very hot nor very cold weather.

TO LEARN MORE

FURTHER READINGS

Harvey, Derek. *Super Shark Encyclopedia and Other Creatures of the Deep*. DK Publishing, 2015.

Musgrave, Ruth. *Shark Rescue: All About Sharks and How to Save Them*. National Geographic, 2016.

Skerry, Brian. *The Ultimate Book of Sharks: Your Guide to These Fierce and Fantastic Fish*. National Geographic, 2018.

ONLINE RESOURCES

To learn more about sharks, please visit **abdobooklinks.com** or scan this QR code. These links are routinely monitored and updated to provide the most current information available.

INDEX

Previously titled The Shark Encyclopedia for Kids

First Edition
First Paperback Printing, 2022

THIS BOOK CONTAINS
RECYCLED MATERIALS

Editor: Alyssa Sorenson
Series Designer: Colleen McLaren
Cover Designer: Karli Kruse

ISBN: 978-1-952455-03-2 (paperback)

Library of Congress Control Number: 2020906137

Distributed in paperback by North Star Editions, Inc.
2297 Waters Drive
Mendota Heights, MN 55120
www.northstareditions.com

Printed in the United States of America